EXPLORING CIVIL RIGHTS

HIGH COURT BANS
SEGREGATION IN
PUBLIC SCHOOLS

THE BEGINNINGS
1954

SELENE CASTROVILLA

Franklin Watts®
An imprint of Scholastic Inc.

Content Consultant

A special thank you to Ryan M. Jones at the National Civil Rights Museum for his expert consultation.

Library of Congress Cataloging-in-Publication Data
Names: Castrovilla, Selene, 1966- author.
Title: The beginnings : 1954 / by Selene Castrovilla.
Other titles: Exploring civil rights.
Description: First edition. | New York : Franklin Watts, an imprint of
  Scholastic Inc., 2022. | Series: Exploring civil rights | Includes
  bibliographical references and index. | Audience: Ages 10–14 | Audience:
  Grades 7–9 | Summary: "Series continuation. Narrative nonfiction, key
  events of the Civil Rights Movement in the years spanning from
  1939–1954. Photographs throughout"— Provided by publisher.
Identifiers: LCCN 2022002592 (print) | LCCN 2022002593 (ebook) |
  ISBN 9781338800654 (library binding) | ISBN 9781338800661 (paperback) |
  ISBN 9781338800678 (ebk)
Subjects: LCSH: African Americans—Civil rights—History—20th
  century—Juvenile literature. | Civil rights movements—United
  States—History—20th century—Juvenile literature. | Civil rights
  workers—United States—Juvenile literature. | BISAC: JUVENILE
  NONFICTION / History / United States / 20th Century | JUVENILE
  NONFICTION / History / United States / General
Classification: LCC E185.61 .C2934 2022 (print) | LCC E185.61 (ebook) |
  DDC 323.1196/073—dc23/eng/20220131
LC record available at https://lccn.loc.gov/2022002592
LC ebook record available at https://lccn.loc.gov/2022002593

10 9 8 7 6 5 4 3 2 1   23 24 25 26 27

Printed in China   62
First edition, 2023

Composition by Kay Petronio

COVER & TITLE PAGE: A mother and daughter sit on the Supreme Court steps in May 1954 after segregation in public schools is banned.

Robert Russa Moton High School students strike, pages 42–43.

Table of Contents

INTRODUCTION
The Way It Was 4

1 **Education in Black and White** 8

2 **The Path to Justice** 20

3 **Monumental Victory** 30

4 **Racism in Virginia** 40

5 **A New Evil** 50

6 **Roots of Change** 62

CONCLUSION
The Legacy of 1954 in Civil Rights History 78

Biography CONSTANCE BAKER MOTLEY ... 82
Timeline 88
Glossary 90
Bibliography 92
Index 94
About the Author 96

T. R. M. Howard, page 61.

Lavinia Baker and her children survived an attack by a white mob that killed her husband, Frazer, in North Carolina in 1898.

The Way It Was

In the period directly following the American Civil War (1861–1865), three **amendments** to the U.S. Constitution sought to grant African Americans the rights they'd been denied during slavery. In 1865, the Thirteenth Amendment abolished slavery. In 1868, the Fourteenth Amendment granted **citizenship** to African Americans. And in 1870, the Fifteenth Amendment gave African American men the right to vote.

Despite those triumphs, this period also saw the introduction of Black codes, or laws passed to limit the rights and freedoms of Black Americans. They soon became known as **Jim Crow** laws, and they were especially strict in the American South. Jim Crow laws controlled where people of color could live and work.

Jim Crow laws enforced **segregation**. Under the racial policy of "separate but equal," Black Americans could be given separate facilities if the quality was equal to the white facilities. In reality, however, there was no equality. African Americans were forced to attend separate and inadequate schools, live in run-down neighborhoods, and even drink from rusty or broken public water fountains.

In 1896, a group of **activists** tried to overturn the Jim Crow laws with the Supreme Court case *Plessy v. Ferguson*. Unfortunately, when they lost the case, Jim Crow laws became even more acceptable across the country, but remained most prominent in the southern United States.

The Fight Begins

As Jim Crow expanded, two prominent **civil rights** organizations emerged. The National Association of Colored Women's Clubs (NACWC) was founded in 1896 by a group of politically active women, including Harriet Tubman. Members of the association dedicated themselves to fighting for voting rights and for ending racial violence in the form of **lynchings** against African Americans. In addition to lynchings, African Americans suffered severe harassment, beatings, and even bombings at the hands of racist organizations like the **Ku Klux Klan** (KKK), which had millions of members by the 1920s.

The National Association for the Advancement of Colored People (NAACP), founded in 1909, followed in the NACWC's footsteps. The NAACP focused on opposing segregation and Jim Crow policies. Both organizations would be crucial in the coming fight for justice.

1954

The 1954 Supreme Court decision in the *Brown v. Board of Education of Topeka* case was a combination of lawsuits challenging school segregation in the United States. Fifty-eight years after *Plessy v. Ferguson*, the *Brown* ruling finally put an end to "separate but equal." This decision had a monumental ripple effect and a positive influence on the African American community going forward. As many southern white people were furious about the Court's decision to abolish segregation, reaction in the form of violence and **legislation** to stall school **integration** became the new battleground. The formation of White Citizens' Councils in many southern states aimed to keep Black Americans from gaining equality with white Americans. ■

Linda Brown was refused enrollment to an all-white elementary school in Topeka, Kansas, in 1951.

1

Education in Black and White

In January 1954, the Supreme Court was considering *Brown v. Board of Education of Topeka*—five combined legal cases for **desegregating** American public schools. In 1951, five separate school desegregation cases were heard in Kansas, South Carolina, Delaware, Virginia, and the District of Columbia. Only the Delaware case resulted in a win for the **plaintiff**, but it did not desegregate all Delaware schools. Because the decision did not strike down educational segregation, Thurgood Marshall, a NAACP lawyer, and his legal team appealed to the Supreme Court. The other four cases were appealed as well. The Supreme Court agreed to hear all these cases combined into one, argued under the name *Brown v. Board of Education of Topeka*. The date was set for December 9, 1952.

In 1950, "Mama" Sarah L. Murphy teaches some of her 48 African American students in this run-down Rockmart, Georgia, segregated two-room schoolhouse.

Lawyers would argue each case independently, but there would be one decision rendered for them all. The proceedings were delayed, and it took until the end of 1953 to begin **deliberations**.

As 1954 started and the nation waited for a ruling, there was a split in the African American community where the *Brown* lawsuit originated: Topeka, Kansas.

The Topeka NAACP chapter, which had initiated the case, remained dedicated to integrating schools. But Black teachers and some Black parents were against desegregation. The teachers knew that many of them would lose their jobs if the Black schools closed. It wasn't likely that they would be accepted as teachers for classes with white students. The parents felt that the Black teachers did an outstanding job—a fact that no one disputed. They felt that their children would be harmed by leaving the schools and teachers they were used to.

The parents named in the *Brown* case also loved the teachers, but they felt that the inferiority of the classroom materials and of the classrooms themselves were a larger concern. The Black schools were old and run-down, and the textbooks were tattered hand-me-downs from the

Topeka Superintendent of Schools Wendell R. Godwin.

white schools. Even more urgent was the danger their children faced, being subjected to harsh weather while walking to bus stops when there were schools for white students right in their own neighborhoods.

Wendell R. Godwin, superintendent of Topeka schools, did not wish to be involved in the **controversy** any longer. He had already filed a recommendation that all the city's schools be integrated gradually. Godwin also sent letters to Black teachers informing them that their services would no longer be needed. He wished them well during this "period of adjustment."

Glaring Differences

In 1954 in the U.S., 17 states and the District of Columbia **mandated** the segregation of Black students in public schools. Seventy percent of America's Black population lived in those places. In four other states, segregation was optional though not required. In the remaining 27 states, segregation in the public schools was **prohibited**, or there was no legislation on the subject.

Six of the 20 African American students for whom the Topeka, Kansas, *Brown v. Board of Education* case was brought, with their parents.

Black students eating lunch in a South Carolina "Jimmy Byrnes school," named after Governor Byrnes, who was white.

Southern Desperation

Sensing that educational desegregation was brewing, Alabama had begun equalizing Black and white school funding and teacher pay. By 1954, Black teachers' salaries had increased by nearly 212 percent, and student funding had also increased. State officials felt that if they truly offered a separate but equal educational experience, they could avoid integration. They created "equalization schools" in all of Alabama's 67 counties. In each location, a Black school was modeled identically after a white school, using the most modern architectural ideas for the buildings. They were generally long and low concrete block buildings with brick exteriors.

Black Radio

The first Black-owned radio network was launched on January 20, 1954. The National Negro Network was projected to reach 12 million of the 15 million Black Americans.

The National Negro Network was comprised of 40 charter member radio stations. It featured a variety of programming, such as soap operas and musical shows, including productions by Cab Calloway, a popular jazz performer and actor.

Unfortunately, due to the rising TV era, the network failed within a year for lack of money.

Actress Ruby Dee starred in one of the National Negro Network's more popular shows, *The Story of Ruby Valentine*.

The most important feature was large windows, to allow maximum light and, most importantly in the southern heat, ventilation.

In 1954, Georgia was the first southern state to start a program for equalizing separate schools using a sales tax to pay for new buildings. Strongly against desegregation, Georgia established an independent corporation called the State School Building Authority to manage the construction of hundreds of new schools in Georgia, working with the State Board of Education and local school districts. They used a measurement formula of $7.50 per square foot per student—an equal measurement for

all. Often, these were the first modern schools rural areas had seen—for Black and for white students. The school auditoriums were large enough to seat an entire community. Black teachers were among the highest salary earners in their communities, and the educational **curriculums** of all schools were improved.

James F. Byrnes, governor of South Carolina and a former Supreme Court justice, proclaimed that separation of the races was his primary objective. The state government was particularly on edge because *Briggs v. Elliott*, one of the five *Brown* cases the Supreme Court was deliberating, originated in South Carolina's Clarendon County.

African American students praying at a segregated school in Farmville, Virginia, in 1953.

Oprah Winfrey

Oprah Winfrey was born into rural Mississippi poverty on January 29, 1954. Her mother was a single teenager. Oprah's early years were grim. She went to live with her maternal grandmother in Milwaukee's poor inner city when she was 6, and she became pregnant when she was 14. Her son was born prematurely and died as an infant.

Sent to live in Nashville, Tennessee, with her father, Winfrey's life turned around. She got a radio job while still in high school and became anchor of the evening news at age 19.

Winfrey continued her climb to success by becoming a TV talk show host. Increasingly popular, she became an idol to millions. The nationally syndicated *Oprah Winfrey Show* ran for 25 years, the highest-rated show of its kind in history. Today, Winfrey is the chair and CEO of her own production company. As the richest Black woman in America, she prides herself on helping others.

Oprah Winfrey with two 2011 graduates from the Oprah Winfrey Leadership Academy for Girls in Henley on Klip, South Africa.

Byrnes started a school equalization plan, and the new buildings were often referred to as "Jimmy Byrnes Schools" or "Byrnes Schools." They were also called "separate but equal schools" and "Jim Crow tax schools." This was the first time that South Carolina had ever funded Black schools.

Other states that funded equalization schools were Virginia (home of *Davis v. County School Board of Prince Edward County*, another *Brown* case), Tennessee, and Texas. Louisiana had local programs run by school boards.

A plan for equalization in Mississippi never began. One of the poorest states, Mississippi, did not have the financial means to build schools for Black students that equaled white schools. State officials were divided on what to do: wait and see what the Supreme Court decision would be, or somehow try to equalize. This fight resulted in nothing being done except for Black teachers making a little more money than they had before. ■

Thurgood Marshall arrives on a train in Charleston, South Carolina, in 1951 to prepare for the school desegregation case *Briggs v. Elliott*.

2

The Path to Justice

The Supreme Court was in no rush to rule on the *Brown* case, where there would likely be civil unrest in the wake of their ruling. Five judges, including Chief Justice Fred Vinson, were opposed to ending segregation in schools; four were in favor. The cases were reargued, but before the justices could take their official vote, Chief Justice Vinson died suddenly in 1953. Earl Warren, a governor and attorney general of California, who supported desegregation, replaced Vinson in October.

On January 11, Warren was nominated to be Supreme Court chief justice by President Dwight D. Eisenhower but still had to be confirmed by the Senate. In a heartbeat, educational desegregation in the United States was assured. But how would the southern states react?

Change in Fate

The Supreme Court spent the early months of 1954 in private meetings about *Brown v. Board of Education*.

Warren's nomination changed the fate of the *Brown* case, shifting the balance of the five-to-four-vote split. Warren was deeply distressed by the separation of Black children from their peers. He felt this not only put a mark of inferiority on them in the community but also upon their hearts and minds, a mark that would likely never be erased. Suddenly, Vinson's allies were in the minority. There was no doubt that the plaintiffs in *Brown* would prevail.

Warren had the votes to strike down segregation, but he believed the Court must do so **unanimously** because this would show the country and the world how strongly the Court supported integration.

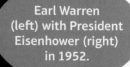

Earl Warren (left) with President Eisenhower (right) in 1952.

Hidden Black Scientists

On February 23, 1954, a group of children from Arsenal Elementary School in Pittsburgh, Pennsylvania, received the first injections of the new **polio** vaccine developed by Dr. Jonas Salk.

Polio had been considered a "white" disease for many years, but the truth was that Black people were not given the same medical care as white people and their polio cases were often not reported or treated. Jim Crow laws kept Black Americans from medical help in many places. The Tuskegee Infantile Paralysis Center at the Tuskegee Institute in Alabama had been established for Black children to be treated by Black doctors.

Black scientists at the Tuskegee Institute provided a missing piece needed for the polio vaccine: HeLa cells. These special cells used in research were named after a Black woman, Henrietta Lacks. The cells were highly sensitive to temperature change—and a rise in temperature would destroy them. Russell W. Brown directed the Tuskegee Institute's HeLa cell project for the Salk polio vaccine, assisted by James H. M. Henderson. The team provided the 10,000 glass tubes of HeLa cells needed for the trials— starting with the Arsenal Elementary School students.

A portrait of Dr. Russell Brown (left) and Dr. James H. M. Henderson (right).

In November 1953, newly appointed Chief Justice Earl Warren (front row, left) stands with President Eisenhower and the Supreme Court justices.

He felt this would avoid massive southern resistance. Although the legal effect would be the same for a majority vote as for a unanimous decision, any votes against *Brown* could be used by segregation supporters as a justification to fight the law and keep the practice of separate education going.

Political Influence

One evening, Eisenhower invited Warren to a White House dinner. He arrived to find John W. Davis, one of the lawyers defending segregation in the *Brown* case, seated nearby. The message was clear: Eisenhower wanted Warren's Court to vote against the *Brown* plaintiffs. After dinner, Eisenhower took Warren aside and told him that southerners were "not bad people." He tried to explain that they just didn't want their children sitting next to Black children in school. Warren was appalled by this remark, and his opinion of the man who had appointed him came crashing down.

The revelation of Eisenhower's racist nature cemented Warren's gut feeling that it was best to wait for a formal meeting to plead his case for a unanimous vote. But he could do something informally. Bringing the justices together as a group was the perfect step toward bringing the votes together. It was not an easy task with men who held different beliefs. He realized that what he had to do was not speak but listen. Everyone needed to feel heard.

Chief Justice Warren (right) is helped into his robes by R. G. Marshall, a year before the historic *Brown* ruling.

The Rise of Thurgood Marshall

Thurgood Marshall began his 25-year career with the NAACP shortly after graduating from law school. He had a private practice and represented the NAACP in a 1935 law school **discrimination** case called *Murray v. Pearson*. In 1936, he became part of the NAACP staff.

At age 32, Marshall won the 1940 U.S. Supreme Court case *Chambers v. Florida*. That same year, he founded and became the executive director of the NAACP Legal Defense and Educational Fund and began arguing many civil rights cases in front of the Supreme Court. The *Brown* case was his most historic.

Marshall went on to become a Supreme Court justice himself. He was confirmed on August 30, 1967.

A portrait of Thurgood Marshall, Associate Justice of the Supreme Court.

John W. Davis (left) argued for segregation against Thurgood Marshall (right).

Nurturing Unity

Warren began a campaign to slowly lead the justices into unity. He lunched with the four justices who opposed desegregation, sometimes alone and sometimes with one or two justices who supported desegregation. The idea was to have friendly conversation and give the opposing justices a chance to voice their concerns and come to terms with the fact that desegregation was going to happen.

Sometimes Warren brought all the justices together for lunch. Gradually, the conversations between Warren and the holdout justices shifted. The justices now spoke of segregation in the past tense and talked about how they would mend the country. But while they accepted that they were not going to have their way—school segregation was ending—they did not say they were going to change their votes.

Warren knew that something would have to give to achieve a unanimous vote. What would he have to compromise to win over those four opposing justices? ■

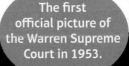

The first official picture of the Warren Supreme Court in 1953.

Perched on the Supreme Court steps after the 1954 segregation ruling, Nettie Hunt explains what this means to her three-and-a-half-year-old daughter Nikie.

3

Monumental Victory

All of America waited for the *Brown* ruling. Eleven-year-old Linda Brown, daughter of Oliver Brown, the named plaintiff in *Brown v. Board of Education*, said that time stood still as her family waited. They were caught in the calm of the hurricane's eye, gazing out at the storm, and wondering how it would all end.

Chief Justice Warren was confirmed by the Senate on March 1. Safely in his seat for life, he assembled a meeting of the justices he had formed friendships with. It was time for him to speak.

Warren presented his fellow justices with the simple argument that the only reason to sustain segregation was an honest belief in the inferiority of Black people. Warren further argued that the Supreme Court must overturn its 1896 ruling that schools may be "separate but equal" to maintain its legitimacy as an institution.

No Vote

The justices opposed to desegregation knew they were outvoted. But Warren had been taking them to lunch and chatting them up since he arrived, looking for something to give them in exchange for their votes. They agreed to withhold stating their positions until the testimony had been discussed as much as possible. They would not take a vote until they knew there was nothing further to say.

All but one of the justices—Stanley Reed—were personally against segregation, but they felt it was up to the states to decide for themselves.

Associate Supreme Court Justice Stanley Reed, from Kentucky, believed in segregated public schools.

Jazz in 1954

Ella Fitzgerald, sometimes called the First Lady of Song, Queen of Jazz, and Lady Ella, recorded her album *Songs in a Mellow Mood* on March 29–30, 1954.

Miles Davis finished recording his album *Blue Haze* on April 3, 1954. A trumpeter, bandleader, and composer, Davis was and still is one of the most respected and celebrated musicians in jazz history.

Louis Armstrong recorded *Louis Armstrong Plays W. C. Handy* on July 12–14, 1954. A trumpeter and singer, Armstrong was and remains beloved and respected in the history of jazz. His career spanned five decades and various jazz eras.

On July 17–18, 1954, the first Newport Jazz Festival was held in Newport, Rhode Island. Almost all the headline performers were African American: the Dizzy Gillespie Quintet, Billie Holiday, Oscar Peterson, Ella Fitzgerald, and Erroll Garner.

Ella Fitzgerald's musical career spanned almost 60 years.

To win these justices' votes, Warren agreed to give the states ample, even unlimited, time to desegregate their schools. The Supreme Court ruling would not include a timeline for the process of desegregation in America.

Warren then spoke with Justice Reed. Educational segregation was ending, Warren said. Reed was alone. Would offering an opposing opinion serve the country, or would it open the door for more division and chaos? Reed agreed to join the majority.

Warren drafted the Court's opinion. The justices met to discuss *Brown* for the last time on Saturday, May 15. Approving the final draft of *Brown*, they agreed to tell no one that they were about to reveal their decision.

Scottswood Bolling and his mother, Sarah, read the *Brown* result in the newspaper the day after the ruling. He was a plaintiff in *Bolling v. Sharpe,* one of the *Brown* cases filed in the District of Columbia.

The Brown Decision Is Announced

At 12:52 p.m. on Monday, May 17, 1954, Chief Justice Warren read the Court's decision to integrate schools. For several minutes, he recapped history: the Fourteenth Amendment, *Plessy v. Ferguson*, and cases since *Plessy* that paved the path toward desegregation. Now, the path was completed.

"We unanimously conclude that in the field of public education the doctrine of 'separate but equal' has no place," Warren declared. The word "unanimous" was not in the actual document—he added it to his speech so there would be no mistaking the Court's unity.

General Benjamin Oliver Davis, Jr.

United States Air Force General Benjamin Oliver Davis, Jr., was promoted to brigadier general on October 27, 1954. Davis was the son of the first African American to achieve the rank of brigadier general in any branch of the U.S. military and the leader of the famed Tuskegee Airmen during World War II. Davis had always resented segregation, but he never let this feeling interfere with his duties to serve his country. Wearing three stars when he retired, Davis was awarded a fourth star by President Bill Clinton in 1998, advancing to full general.

Benjamin Oliver Davis, Jr., broke the color barrier in the U.S. Air Force when he became its first African American brigadier general.

Linda Brown (left) was already in a desegregated junior high school when the Supreme Court reached its verdict.

From the audience, Thurgood Marshall stared in shock at Justice Reed, who gave him the slightest nod from the bench. Reed wiped a tear from his eye.

Reactions

Leola Brown, wife of plaintiff Oliver Brown, was in her Topeka home, ironing, when the decision came over the radio. Her husband felt that the decision would bring a better understanding of race relations, but he worried about the future of Black teachers, who needed support. The Browns' daughter Linda, who at age eight had been refused admission into the local white school, was happy that her sister would

George E. C. Hayes (left), Thurgood Marshall (center), and James M. Nabrit, Jr., stand victorious outside the U.S. Supreme Court.

not have to walk as far to school as she had. Linda was entering junior high school in the fall, which had already been integrated.

In fact, Topeka had already begun planning its elementary school integration. Still, the Topeka NAACP was thrilled for the nationwide victory for civil rights. McKinley Burnett, Topeka NAACP president, and the man who set the case in motion by attending school board meetings for two years and demanding desegregation, thanked God for the Supreme Court. Lucinda Todd, the very first *Brown* plaintiff, said that they had a long way before segregation would be abolished, but she was thankful they had come this far.

Justices Harold H. Burton, Felix Frankfurter, and William O. Douglas each wrote thank-you notes to Warren that day, expressing their joy, relief, and thankfulness for his achievement. Burton told Warren, "To you goes the credit for . . . the all important unanimity."

A young pastor heard the news in Alabama. Dr. Martin Luther King, Jr., saw this as a defining moment. He declared, "To all men of goodwill, this decision came as a joyous daybreak to end the long night of human captivity . . . . It was a reaffirmation of the good old American doctrine of freedom and equality for all men." ■

Joy Cabarrus Speakes reflects back on the poor conditions of her all-Black high school in Prince Edward County, Virginia.

4

Racism in Virginia

Joy Cabarrus Speakes was 12 years old when she joined 16-year-old Barbara Johns and the rest of the 450 Robert Russa Moton High School students who went on strike in 1951. The students' walkout initiated *Dorothy E. Davis v. Prince Edward County,* one of the five *Brown* cases. Living in Farmville, Virginia, had gotten harder in the past four years for Speakes's family and the other families involved with the lawsuit. They had been harassed and were victims of violence. The Johns's home was burned to the ground. A cross was burned on the school's lawn. As a student, Speakes was over-joyed when the Supreme Court ruling was handed down. But other African Americans in Farmville worried that they would be targeted. Would they be able to sell their crops? Would stores and banks continue to give them credit? Speakes and the rest of the Black community of Prince Edward County never imagined the massive resistance southern white citizens would begin to mount against educational integration.

Warren could not imagine it either. He had unity on the Court, but President Eisenhower did not lend his endorsement to the decision. Eisenhower stated

that he had sworn to uphold the country's constitutional process, and he would obey the ruling. This was a far cry from standing with the Court's decision. He privately thought the Court would stay hands off and allow local courts to make their own choices about following the decision.

Some of the more than 100 students who walked out of Robert Russa Moton High School in 1951.

Southern Fury

The southern states' government officials were furious that they had spent so much money on their equalization plans, only to face this ruling. But the fact that they had no directive on timing was their silver lining.

On the floor of **Congress**, Mississippi representative John Bell Williams dubbed May 17, the day of the Brown ruling, "Black Monday."

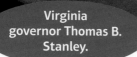

Virginia governor Thomas B. Stanley.

Virginia governor Thomas B. Stanley made a statement on May 18 calling for "cool heads, calm study, and sound judgment." He felt that Virginia could avoid obeying the ruling if a thorough and thoughtful resistance was plotted. Citizens disagreed.

Stanley remained calm but made sure to act quickly. On June 25, he announced that he would use every legal means at his command to continue segregated schools in Virginia. He promised that schools would remain segregated for the 1954–1955 school year.

Hernandez v. Texas

On May 3, 1954, the Supreme Court ruled unanimously that Mexican Americans and all other nationality groups in the United States have equal protection under the U.S. Constitution's Fourteenth Amendment. Chief Justice Earl Warren wrote the decision. It was the first time Mexican American lawyers had appeared before the Supreme Court. Until this ruling, only white and Black citizens could claim civil rights protection under the Fourteenth Amendment. Now, with this ruling, any **ethnic** or nationality group targeted for discrimination would be shielded by the amendment.

Attorneys Gustavo Garcia (left) and John J. Herrera (right) successfully argued that the civil rights of Pete Hernandez (center) had been violated during his murder trial.

A Black student takes a drink in a segregated, run-down Farmville, Virginia, high school.

Virginia state senator Garland Gray.

Senator Harry F. Byrd.

The Gray Commission

Five days before Stanley's announcement, 20 Virginia legislators had met in a firehouse at the invitation of state senator Garland Gray. They reported back to Stanley that they had declared themselves "unalterably opposed" to racial integration in the schools.

Building on this meeting, Stanley established the 32-member Commission on Public Education on August 23, which would become known as the Gray Commission. The commission's purpose was to study the effects of the Supreme Court *Brown* decision and to make recommendations. One major thing the commission researched was the possibility of ending funds for public education in Virginia and offering grants to white parents to send their children to private schools. Senator Harry F. Byrd also declared his opposition to desegregating Virginia's schools.

First and Last

The Greensboro, North Carolina, school board announced on May 18, 1954, that it would abide by the *Brown* ruling. It was the first city in the South to agree to follow the law—and for years it was the only one. But some Greensboro citizens opposed and fought integration, blocking its implementation. In 1969, the **federal** government discovered that the city was not in **compliance** with the 1964 Civil Rights Act that had outlawed racial discrimination. Transitioning to an integrated school system did not start until 1971, due to lawsuits and both nonviolent and violent protests. While Greensboro rushed to prove itself as **progressive**, it became one of the last educationally integrated cities in the South.

On September 3, 1957, five Black students are escorted by police past protestors to attend classes at the previously segregated Gillespie Park School in Greensboro.

In 1959, protestors at the Arkansas state capitol still fought against the enrollment of African American students.

Soon he would mastermind a massive resistance in which all the southern states would team together against integration. Part of this resistance would occur later in Congress, with 82 representatives and 19 senators from southern states signing the Southern **Manifesto** of 1956, slamming the *Brown* decision as an unlawful abuse of power and a violation of states' rights. ∎

SAVE
SEGREGATION
VOTE

STATES
RIGHTS
PLEDGED
ELECTORS

Members of the
White Citizens' Council
of Greater New Orleans
protest the integration of two
local elementary schools in
November 1960.

5

A New Evil

To Mississippi officials, the Supreme Court decision might as well have been a declaration of war. The minimal measures they had taken to equalize education—or anything else, like voting—were dropped and the fight against desegregation and civil rights was on.

Massive Resistance

Mississippi governor Hugh Lawson White made one attempt to negotiate with African American civil rights leaders. At a meeting in July, White offered to build separate Black schools equal to white ones if the idea of desegregation was off the table. The leaders rejected this plan and declared their intention of seeing *Brown* carried out. White then abandoned trying to negotiate, joining the vocal white citizens and elected officials who

Mississippi governor Hugh Lawson White.

were determined to fight the federal attack on educational segregation—using whatever means necessary.

White immediately declared "massive resistance" an official policy, and he and the state legislature plotted to legally block all attempts for civil rights.

Racist Amendments

White called a special legislative session to pass an amendment to Mississippi's constitution: The state could eliminate public schools in any districts attempting to desegregate. The legislature also hindered Black voter registration by passing another amendment stating that a voter must be able to not only read a document, but also **interpret** it. This was vague enough that registrars could easily use it as a reason to stop African Americans from registering. Voters approved these two amendments. Re-registration campaigns were created on the county level, forcing Black citizens to apply for the right to vote under the new measures.

In August, the Walthall County, Virginia, branch of the NAACP submitted a school desegregation petition. In response, local authorities closed the county's

In Atlanta, Georgia, African Americans line up to register to vote despite the obstacles in their way.

Black schools for two weeks. They also fired school employees suspected of being involved with the petition.

White Supremacist Citizens

While White met with Black leaders in a failed negotiation, white citizens were forming a white supremacist organization to fight *Brown*. The White Citizens' Council was established on July 11 in Indianola, a small Mississippi town. Robert B. Patterson, a local **plantation** manager and a former Mississippi State University football team captain, was the group's founder. Indianola was a mere 40 miles away from Mound Bayou, where the Regional Council of Negro Leadership (RCNL), a civil rights organization, was located.

Cassius Clay

In October 1954, 12-year-old Cassius Clay was devastated to discover that his new red Schwinn bicycle had been stolen from outside the Columbia Auditorium in Louisville, Kentucky. He was told there was a police officer in the basement, so he went looking for him. That officer, Joe Martin, happened to be a boxing trainer. Clay told Martin, "If I find the guy who took my bike, I'm gonna whup him." Martin responded that in that case, Clay had better know how to fight. He offered to train him.

Clay won his first fight six weeks after beginning training with Martin. Not only did Clay have great strength and speed, but he was quick-thinking and could take a punch without panicking. Clay became a successful amateur boxer, and he won a gold medal in light heavyweight boxing at the 1960 Olympics in Rome, Italy.

Muhammad Ali was also a master of spoken word poetry combined with hip hop, and he received two Grammy nominations.

He turned professional that same year. At age 22 he won the world heavyweight championship in a major upset on February 25, 1964. Two weeks later, on March 6, he announced that he had joined the Black Muslim group Nation of Islam, and he would now be known as Muhammad Ali. In 1966, he refused to be drafted into the Vietnam War, stating his religious and ethical beliefs against war. He lost his right to fight as he appealed his conviction up to the Supreme Court, which overturned the conviction in 1971. Although he lost almost five prime fighting years, he was the first person to win the heavyweight championship three separate times. He successfully defended his title 19 times. He is often ranked as the greatest heavyweight boxer of all time. *Sports Illustrated* magazine named him the greatest sportsman of the 20th century.

Incited to riot by a White Citizens' Council leader, a white mob attacks a car carrying Black passengers in Tennessee.

It was the RCNL that had met with Governor White and rejected his offer for separate but equal schools.

New White Citizens' Council chapters quickly sprang up in Mississippi and the rest of the Deep South. The organization was composed of and supported by the wealthiest and most influential community members: business owners, bankers, lawyers, doctors, newspaper publishers, and law enforcement. Sometimes religious leaders were involved.

The Catch

New York Giants center fielder Willie Mays made what is considered one of the greatest baseball plays in history on September 29, 1954. It was Game 1 of the 1954 World Series against the Cleveland Indians at the Polo Grounds in Upper Manhattan, New York City. In the eighth inning, with runners on bases and the score tied 2–2, Cleveland Indians batter Vic Wertz hit a deep fly ball to center field that should have allowed all the runners to score. But Mays made an incredible over-the-shoulder catch while running, throwing the ball back to the infield to send the Cleveland runners out. The Giants went on to win the game 5–2 and sweep the series.

Willie Mays (left) chats with Tris Speaker, former player for Cleveland, during the 1954 World Series.

What made the Council so dangerous was the fact that its members performed racist acts openly, using their power, personal connections, and money to hurt Black Americans. These were people in high places, trying to crush the spirit of civil rights seekers. They refused bank loans to Black farmers and Black businesses who supported advancement for African Americans. They also evicted Black renters who strove for equality, and terminated Black employees belonging to civil rights organizations. Council members claimed to be against violence, but the environment they created helped the Ku Klux Klan flourish and increase membership in the South.

The KKK often worked with southern police departments and government officials in an effort to terrorize and keep Black citizens oppressed.

Black Monday

On October 28, Thomas Pickens Brady, a Council member and Mississippi Circuit Court judge, delivered an address called "Black Monday" to the Sons of the American Revolution in Greenwood, Mississippi. This speech detailed the belief that African Americans were inferior to Europeans and the races must remain separate. It called for the abolishment of the NAACP, the creation of a separate state for Black Americans, and the elimination of public schools. It was so well received that Brady gave the copyright to the Council, which published it as a pamphlet, charging $1 per copy.

Carmen Jones Is Released

Carmen Jones, an American musical film, was released on October 28, 1954, and starred Dorothy Dandridge and Harry Belafonte, the popular folk singer, civil rights activist, and friend of Martin Luther King, Jr. Based on a Broadway show and the opera *Carmen*, this movie earned Dandridge the first African American Oscar nomination for Best Actress in a leading role. Because Dandridge and Belafonte did not sing opera, they were "voiced over," or replaced, by opera singers for the songs in the film.

Dorothy Dandridge and Harry Belafonte in *Carmen Jones*, which won the Golden Globe Award for Best Motion Picture—Musical or Comedy.

In addition to his work as a civil rights leader, T. R. M. Howard was a surgeon and a successful businessman.

The proceeds earned the Council enough funds to continue to operate. The Council also started publishing a newsletter in October.

Fighting the Council

T. R. M. Howard, cofounder of the Regional Council of Negro Leadership, lashed back at the White Citizens' Council with a plan to economically protect the Black citizens in Mississippi. He suggested the NAACP encourage all Black-owned and Black-run Mississippi businesses, churches, and associations to transfer their accounts to the Tri-State Bank of Memphis, which was also Black-owned. The bank provided loans to victims of the Council's financial assault in Mississippi. ∎

Two years after integrating into a formerly white school, Hugh Price became a cadet at Coolidge High School.

6

Roots of Change

The September school year brought change to the District of Columbia, where one of the *Brown* lawsuits had originated. The superintendent of schools in Washington, DC, Hobart Corning, planned a gradual integration in two waves of students. The first wave, that September, would be small. It would consist of Black students who had not been a part of the city's public school system before. Either they had moved from another area or had gone to private schools.

Hugh Price was one of the "firsts." The Black eighth grader had been enrolled in an integrated private school when the *Brown* decision was announced. Now, going to Taft Junior High School as one of 26 African American students in a student body of 850, he felt tense. He and his Black classmates at the private school had been used as punching bags by white students more than once

Price's teacher at Taft decided to make all the Black students hall monitors. This backfired, making the new students easy targets between classes. They were punched, poked, nudged. Still, Price thought the first week went well.

The first integration wave went so well that Corning decided to push up the second wave. The Black students would arrive on October 4. White parents were up in arms, and white students walked out of school in protest. Price and a handful of other Black students were actually invited by the white students to walk out with them.

Army Desegregated

On October 30, 1954, the Department of Defense announced that the United States armed forces had been fully desegregated. It had been six years since President Harry S. Truman issued Executive Order 9981. Signed on July 26, 1948, the order mandated the racial integration of America's armed forces. The September 1954 deactivation of the 94th Engineer Battalion, the army's last all-Black unit, completed the long process.

Black units like the 24th Infantry Regiment were still operating during the Korean War (1950–1953).

14

It didn't take much to get the white students back in school. Threatened with the loss of after-school clubs, music and drama programs, and sports, they gave up their fight and settled back to the business of school. Price was never embraced by the white students, but he was no longer harassed.

Integration in the District of Columbia had been accomplished fairly easily—unlike in neighboring Virginia, where it would not happen for years to come.

In nearby Baltimore, Maryland, plans to integrate were underway. Located on the Mason-Dixon line, where the South begins, Baltimore ignored pressure from white southerners to maintain segregation. It would begin in September 1955.

The Milford Eleven

Delaware was another *Brown* lawsuit location. Following the Supreme Court's ruling, the Delaware State Board of Education issued a notice to local

One of eleven Black students exits Milford High School with no trouble from his white peers.

schools: They needed to have a plan for desegregation in place by October 1. The schools rejected this date. Some districts said they needed 12 years to integrate.

But one Delaware school, Milford High School, attempted to integrate in September by admitting 11 African American students. Orlando Camp was one of those students. He wanted to attend Milford not for integration, but for opportunity. The formerly white school had much more to offer him than the Black school he had attended.

Charles Diggs, Jr.

In November, Charles Diggs, Jr., became Michigan's first
African American elected to Congress. Diggs was devoted to
the civil rights movement. In April 1955, he spoke to about
10,000 people at the annual conference of the Regional
Council of Negro Leadership in Mound Bayou, Mississippi. He
also attended the trial of the accused murderers of Emmett
Till, a Black teenager who was murdered during a trip to
Mississippi. While in Mississippi, Diggs was subjected to
Jim Crow segregation laws, even though he was a member
of Congress. Upon his return to Washington, DC, Diggs
asked President Eisenhower to convene a special session of
Congress to discuss civil rights. He later became a founding
member and the first chair of the Congressional Black
Caucus, a group of Black members of Congress working to
better represent their Black **constituents**.

Charles Diggs, Jr., shakes hands with
Speaker of the House Sam Rayburn,
just after Diggs is sworn in.

Two African American students get picked up after attending classes at Milford High School.

Camp's mother sent him to Strawbridge & Clothier in Philadelphia to buy new school clothes. She wanted him to look his best for this opportunity. She knew he would act his best.

The first day was fine. The 686 white students were cordial enough—but then those students went home and told their parents about the Black kids in their classes.

Protests began at the school. On the third day, 300–400 people stood at the door, calling Camp and his fellow African American students names.

Louis Redding, the Black attorney who had argued and won two Delaware desegregation cases that became part of the *Brown* decision, stepped in. The Milford police would not help, so Redding called the Delaware State Police to escort the 11 students to school. The state police drove them each day, but the mobs kept coming. They threw things at the students and stayed outside all day.

The situation escalated when a white supremacist named Bryant William Bowles, Jr., arrived on the scene. He riled up the crowds with racist speeches, and cross burnings began. Could an eruption of violence be close behind?

A September 1954 protest of Milford High School's desegregation.

On October 3, 1954, white citizens attend a mass rally celebrating Milford High's failure to integrate.

White students began staying home. Camp and the rest of the Milford Eleven continued to attend classes, but they realized that this probably wasn't going to last.

They were right. In less than a month, the Delaware Supreme Court ruled that though the Milford school district had acted legally, it had acted too fast. The 11 Black students were transferred out of Milford High School. Camp wound up at William Henry High School in Dover, an all-Black public school 20 miles away.

Different Views

Ruth Ann Scales.

Vivian Scales.

Fourteen-year-old Ruth Ann Scales, daughter of Topeka, Kansas, plaintiff Vivian Scales, felt that integration was not that great. She preferred school before desegregation, when she could be with all her friends. Her parents had wanted equality, but Scales felt that their lives didn't change after the Supreme Court decision. They had reached one milestone but there was so much more. Everything else in Topeka was still segregated: restaurants, stores, hotels, and public transportation. After the ruling she went to school with some white students, but it wasn't a big deal. People were under the impression that all Black students were desperate to go to school with white students, but for her, that wasn't the case.

Katherine Carper, the only student who testified at the original *Brown* trial, felt scared and lonely when she entered an integrated school without her friends. Most of the students were white. Luckily, Mary—a red-haired white girl who wore glasses—approached her. Mary's friend Janice came along. They quickly bonded, eating lunch together on the school lawn. Soon there were other white students with whom she became friendly. Carper learned

Katherine Carper went on to graduate from Topeka High School.

two valuable lessons from that time. Standing up in court taught her never to be afraid to tell the truth. And going to an integrated school taught her we should never choose our friends by the color of their skin because we might miss the opportunity for a great friendship.

Stonewalling Desegregation

In South Carolina, the school equalization plan had been paused because Governor Byrnes worried that the state would eventually be forced into desegregation. But he reinstated the program and doubled down on his opposition to integration.

The named plaintiffs in *Briggs v. Elliott*—South Carolina's case in *Brown*—had not fared well. Harry and Eliza Briggs lost their jobs. Harry went

Harry Briggs, Jr., (second row, far right) at his segregated school in South Carolina.

to Florida to find work to support his family, and the children were sent to New York to live with relatives.

Threats of Violence

In West Virginia, 25 counties integrated schools in September, following the instructions of State Superintendent of Schools W. W. Trent. But Black students entering White Sulphur Springs

West Virginia Superintendent of Schools W. W. Trent.

High School in Greenbrier County were threatened with bodily harm. The Greenbrier County Board of Education canceled integration and ordered that the students attend the schools they did the year prior. Trent refused to interfere because boards of education were free to refuse integration at that time. West Virginia NAACP Charleston Branch president Willard A. Brown spoke to African Americans at the White Sulphur Springs Baptist Church about this situation on September 14. During the meeting, white protestors terrorized the people inside the church, shutting off the lights and firing guns outside. ■

Originally named The Ashmun Institute, Lincoln University was established in Pennsylvania on April 29, 1854. Located in Chester County, this was the country's first degree-granting historically Black college and university (HBCU).

James Ralston Amos, a 28-year-old African American farmer, sparked pastor John Miller Dickey's idea to create a higher-learning institution for African American men. Amos wanted to attend college, but none would accept him. Dickey, along with his wife, Sarah Emlen Cresson, planned the institute. Amos promoted attending the new school with residents of Hinsonville, a nearby community

Famed civil rights activists, Dr. Mary McLeod Bethune (left), and W. E. B. Du Bois (center), with Lincoln University President Dr. Horace Mann Bond in 1950.

A sketch of the chapel at Lincoln University from 1895.

of free African Americans where he lived. He also helped raise funding for the school. Amos and other Hinsonville residents built the first structure on the campus.

Amos and his brother, Thomas Henry Amos, became the institute's first graduates, along with Armistead Hutchinson Miller. The three men became ministers and decided to work in Africa. The Ashmun Institute was renamed in honor of Abraham Lincoln in 1866.

Civil rights lawyer and Supreme Court justice Thurgood Marshall was one of Lincoln University's many notable graduates.

LINCOLN UNIVERSITY
OF
THE COMMONWEALTH SYSTEM OF HIGHER EDUCATION
1972
FOUNDED
1854
LINCOLN UNIVERSITY, PENNSYLVANIA

Schools in Hoxie, Arkansas, integrated in 1955.

The Legacy of 1954 in Civil Rights History

Though the Supreme Court decision was made, deseg-regation had a long way to go. In 1955, the Supreme Court delivered a second order, known as *Brown II,* stating that the *Brown* decision shall be implemented "with all deliberate speed." This was an open state-ment, leaving responsibility on how and when to carry out the Court's order to the states. In some cases, it would take many years and persistent work by the NAACP and other Black civil rights groups, along with local court mandates, for integration to happen. Many southern states were determined to do anything to stop integration, including closing school districts. Virginia's Prince Edward County closed its public schools for five years. The White Citizens' Councils would continue to fight integration as well.

The events at Milford High School pushed Delaware integration back 10 years. But in 2012, over half a century later, Orlando Camp and his fellow Black classmates received honorary diplomas from Milford High School. Calling *Brown* "one of the most landmark decisions this country has ever had," Camp said that we still had a long way to go.

During 1954, racial discrimination and segregation in public housing was also being challenged in court. In the next year it would be outlawed in St. Louis, Missouri, in a landmark case led by two women civil rights lawyers: Frankie Muse Freeman and Constance Baker Motley.

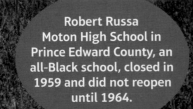

Robert Russa Moton High School in Prince Edward County, an all-Black school, closed in 1959 and did not reopen until 1964.

However, civil rights in the United States became rooted by the 1954 *Brown* decision. The monumental ruling continued to inspire activists as the movement grew into the second half of the 1950s and gained even more strength in the 1960s.

Reflecting on all that the *Brown* decision triggered, Joy Cabarrus Speakes regretted none of the hardships that she and other Black students endured in Prince Edward County afterward—and she was proud of going on strike with Barbara Johns. She said that the difference between a moment and a movement is sacrifice. ■

In St. Louis, Missouri, a bronze statue of Frankie Muse Freeman honors the civil rights attorney.

Constance Baker Motley

Constance Baker Motley was a Black woman of firsts. In 1946, she became the first female lawyer for the NAACP Legal Defense and Educational Fund (LDF), and in 1950 she wrote the original complaint for *Brown v. Board of Education*. She became the first African American female lawyer to argue a case before the Supreme Court, eventually arguing 10 cases before the Court and winning nine. She was the first female New York state senator, the first woman and first African American borough president of Manhattan in New York City, and the first Black woman to serve as a federal judge.

Constance Baker Motley is sworn in as the first woman elected Manhattan Borough president on February 25, 1965.

Born in New Haven, Connecticut, on September 14, 1921, Constance Baker was the ninth of 12 children. Her parents, Rachel and McCullough Baker, were immigrants from Nevis, a Caribbean island. Rachel Baker became a community activist, founding the New Haven NAACP.

Already aware of social injustice, 15-year-old Constance read the writings of civil rights leaders James Weldon Johnson and W. E. B. Du Bois, and their words inspired her to learn about Black history. She took classes with a minister who taught her about the roots of the civil rights movement, and she learned that

Baker Motley chats with Dr. Martin Luther King, Jr., in 1965.

Baker's activism flourished in high school. She became president of the New Haven Negro Youth Council and secretary of the New Haven Adult Community Council. She graduated with honors but could not afford college. A local businessman named Clarence W. Blakeslee heard her speak at a local community center and offered to pay for her education. This act of kindness stayed in Baker's heart. She realized the importance of compassion and

Black lawyers were underrepresented. Constance heard an inner call to become an attorney for civil rights.

Baker Motley walks with James Meredith (right), who she represented in his lawsuit to be the first black student at the University of Mississippi.

developed a belief that one dedicated person could make a difference in the world.

Riding a train to Fisk University, a historically Black college in Nashville, Tennessee, Baker experienced Jim Crow laws. Forced to enter a rusty old car labeled COLORED, she wrote, "Although I had known this would happen, I was both frightened and humiliated. All I knew for sure was that I could do nothing about this new reality."

Baker later returned north to attend New York University, where she earned her bachelor of arts degree in 1943. She entered Columbia Law School, receiving her bachelor of laws in 1946. She married real estate and insurance broker Joel Motley, Jr., that same year.

Even before she had graduated from law school, Thurgood Marshall hired Motley to work as a law clerk at the LDF. Once she earned her degree, she

Baker Motley makes a victory sign two days after her election as the first African American woman to serve in the New York State Senate.

became the first woman on his legal team. She experienced **prejudice** from men in court who did not respect women as lawyers. Sometimes judges turned their backs on her as she spoke. Motley didn't let this behavior affect her. She wrote in her autobiography, "I was the kind of person who would not be put down."

Motley's life was in constant danger when she went down

South to work on cases. Hotels didn't allow Black guests, so local activists hosted her. She had trouble sleeping, even when armed men stood guard at her door. One of her hosts, Mississippi's Medgar Evers, was assassinated in his driveway in 1963. Motley also represented Dr. Martin Luther King, Jr. She was awed by his willingness to die for African Americans' freedom.

In 1964, Motley was elected to the New York State Senate. The following year, she was chosen as Manhattan borough president. On January 26, 1966, President Lyndon B. Johnson nominated Motley to a seat on the United States District Court for the Southern District of New York. Her United States Senate confirmation was delayed for seven months by Senator James Eastland of Mississippi, who objected to her past desegregation work. Finally,

"We Americans entered a new phase in our history—the era of integration—in 1954."

—CONSTANCE BAKER MOTLEY

on August 30, 1966, the Senate confirmed Motley, and she became the first female African American federal judge.

From 1982 to 1986, she served as chief judge, and remained on the bench until her death on September 28, 2005.

During her years as a federal judge, Motley continued to work for equal rights. She received many awards, including the Presidential Citizens Medal, the NAACP's Spingarn Medal (their highest honor), and the Congressional Gold Medal. She is also honored in the National Women's Hall of Fame. Vice President Kamala Harris names Motley as her inspiration.

Determined to achieve her goals regardless of obstacles, Constance Baker Motley proved that one dedicated person *can* make a difference in the world.

82-year-old Judge Constance Baker Motley in her Federal court chambers, May 7, 2004.

TIMELINE

The Year in Civil Rights

1954

MARCH 1

Chief Justice Earl Warren is confirmed by the Senate, securing his place on the Supreme Court for life.

JANUARY 20

The National Negro Network, the first Black-owned radio network, is launched.

FEBRUARY 23

A group of children from Arsenal Elementary School in Pittsburgh, Pennsylvania, receive the first injections of the new polio vaccine, developed with help from Black scientists at the Tuskegee Institute.

MAY 3

The Supreme Court rules unanimously that Mexican Americans and all other nationality groups in the United States have equal protection under the U.S. Constitution's Fourteenth Amendment.

MAY 17

The Supreme Court rules in favor of the plaintiffs in the *Brown* case, banning segregation in public schools.

Milford High School in Delaware attempts to integrate by admitting 11 African American students.

JULY 11

The White Citizens' Council is established in Indianola, Mississippi, to fight against the *Brown* ruling.

JULY 17–18

The first Newport Jazz Festival is held in Newport, Rhode Island. Almost all the headline performers were African American, including Ella Fitzgerald.

OCTOBER 28

Carmen Jones, an American musical film, is released and stars African American actors Dorothy Dandridge and Harry Belafonte.

OCTOBER 30

The Department of Defense announces that the United States armed forces has been fully desegregated.

AUGUST 23

Virginia governor, Thomas B. Stanley, establishes the Gray Commission to oppose integration in schools.

NOVEMBER

Charles Diggs, Jr., becomes Michigan's first African American elected to Congress.

GLOSSARY

activist (AK-tuh-vist) a person who works to bring about political or social change

amendment (uh-MEND-muhnt) a change that is made to a law or legal document

citizenship (SIT-i-zuhn-ship) the legal status of being a citizen of a country, with full rights to live, work, and vote there

civil rights (SIV-uhl rites) the individual rights that all members of a democratic society have to freedom and equal treatment under the law

compliance (kahm-PLY-ans) the act or process of doing what you have been asked or ordered to do

Congress (KAHN-gris) the lawmaking body of the United States, made up of the Senate and the House of Representatives

constituent (kuhn-STICH-oo-uhnt) a voter represented by an elected official

controversy (KAHN-truh-vur-see) an argument in which people express strongly opposing views about something

curriculum (kuh-RIK-yuh-luhm) an organized program of study in a school or college

deliberation (di-lib-ur-AY-shuhn) the act of considering something carefully

desegregate (dee-SEG-ruh-gayt) to do away with the practice of separating people of different races in schools, restaurants, and other public places

discrimination (dis-krim-uh-NAY-shuhn) prejudice or unfair behavior to others based on differences such as in race, gender, or age

ethnic (ETH-nik) of or having to do with a group of people sharing the same national origins, language, or culture

federal (FED-ur-uhl) national government, as opposed to state or local government

integration (in-ti-GRAY-shuhn) the act or practice of making facilities or an organization open to people of all races and ethnic groups

interpret (in-TUR-prit) to figure out what something means

Jim Crow (jim kro) the practice of segregating Black people in the United States, named after a character who degraded African American life and culture

Ku Klux Klan (KOO kluks KLAN) a secret organization in the United States that uses threats and violence to achieve its goal of white supremacy; also called the Klan or the KKK

legislation (lej-is-LAY-shuhn) laws that have been proposed or made

lynching (LIN-ching) a sometimes public murder by a group of people, often involving hanging

mandate (MAN-date) a task or policy that an elected official has to carry out

manifesto (man-uh-FES-toe) a written statement that describes the policies, goals, and opinions of a person or group

plaintiff (PLAYN-tif) a person who brings a legal action

plantation (plan-TAY-shuhn) a large farm found in warm climates where crops such as coffee, rubber, and cotton are grown

polio (POH-lee-oh) an infectious viral disease that attacks the brain and spinal cord

prejudice (PREJ-uh-dis) immovable, unreasonable, or unfair opinion about someone based on the person's race, religion, or other characteristic

progressive (pruh-GRES-iv) in favor of improvement, progress, or reform, especially in political or social matters

prohibit (proh-HIB-it) to forbid or ban something officially

segregation (seg-ruh-GAY-shuhn) the act or practice of keeping people or groups apart

unanimously (yoo-NAN-uh-muhs-lee) agreed on by everyone

BIBLIOGRAPHY

Booth, Lance. "Overlooked No More: Barbara Johns, Who Defied Segregation in Schools." *The New York Times*, May 8, 2019.

Brown Henderson, Cheryl, Darren Canady, Deborah Dandridge, John Edgar Tidwell, and Vincent Omni. *Recovering Untold Stories: An Enduring Legacy of the Brown v. Board of Education Decision*. Kansas: University of Kansas Libraries, 2018.

Camp, Orlando J. and Ed Kee, eds. *The Milford Eleven*. Delaware: *Delaware Today*, 2021.

Celotto, Bryce. "Bolling v. Sharpe and Beyond: The Unfinished and Untold History of School Desegregation in Washington, D.C." University of Massachusetts Thesis, 2016.

Crowther, Bosley. "Up-dated Translation of Bizet Work Bows." *The New York Times*, October 29, 1954.

Flood, Don. "History of Milford Eleven helped form Delaware's present." Delaware: *Cape Gazette*, 2014.

74 Million, the74million.org

Boundary Stones, boundarystones.weta.org

Brown Foundation for Educational Equity, Excellence and Research, brownvboard.org

C-Span, c-span.org

Civil Rights Digital Library, crdl.usg.edu

Kansas Historical Society, Lucinda Wilson Todd Collection, kshs.org

Library of Congress, loc.gov

Library of Virginia, lva.virginia.gov

Robert Russa Moton Museum, motonmuseum.org

Smithsonian, americanhistory.si.edu

Washington Area Spark, washingtonareaspark.com

A 1953 photograph of some of the students who walked out of Robert Russa Moton High School to demand improvements for their segregated facility.

INDEX

Ali, Muhammad, 54, *54*, 55, *55*
Armstrong, Louis, 33

Baker, Frazer, 4
Baker, Lavinia, *4*
Baker, McCullough, 83
Baker, Rachel, 83
Belafonte, Harry, 60, *60*
Blakeslee, Clarence W., 84
Boddie, Kimber, *35*
Bolling, Sarah, *34*
Bolling, Scottswood, *34*
Bolling v. Sharpe, *34*
Bowles, Bryant William, Jr., 70
Briggs, Eliza, 73
Briggs, Harry, 73, 75
Briggs, Harry, Jr., *74*
Briggs v. Elliott, 17, *20*, 73
Brown, Leola, 37
Brown, Linda, *8*, 31, 37, *37*
Brown, Oliver, 31, 37
Brown, Russell W., 23, *23*
Brown, Willard A., 75
Brown II decision, 79
Brown v. Board of Education
    plaintiffs in, *12–13*, 31, *34*, 37, 39
    and Thurgood Marshall, 9, 26, 37, *38*
    unanimous decision for, 22, 24–29, 31–32, 34–35, 37, 39
Burnett, McKinley, 39
Byrd, Harry F., 47, *47*
Byrnes, James F., *14*, 17, 19, 73

Camp, Orlando, 67, 69, 71, 79–80
Carmen Jones (movie), 60, *60*
Carper, Katherine, 72–73, *73*
Civil Rights Act (1964), 48
Clay, Cassius (later Muhammad Ali), 54–55
Congressional Black Caucus, 68
Corning, Hobart, 63–64, *66*

Dandridge, Dorothy, 60, *60*
Davis, Benjamin Oliver, Jr., 36, *36*
Davis, John W., 24, *27*
Davis, Miles, 33
Dee, Ruby, *15*

desegregation, 7, 9, 21, 27, 32, 34–35, 39, *78*, 86
    and Black teacher job losses, 11–12, 37
    implementation of, 63–64, *64*, 66–67, 69, *69*, 70–71
    plaintiff loss of jobs, 73, 75
    racist amendments against, 7, 52–53
    of the U.S. military, 65
    white protest over, 7, 41–42, 44, 47–49, *49–50*, 51–53, 56, 64, 69–70, *70*, 71, *71*, 79
Diggs, Charles, Jr., 68, *68*
Dorothy E. Davis v. Prince Edward County, 41

Eisenhower, Dwight D., 21, *22*, 24, *24*, 25, 42, 68
equalization schools, 14, *14*, 16–17, 19, 44, 73
Evers, Medgar, 86

Fitzgerald, Ella, 33, *33*
Fourteenth Amendment, 5, 35, 45
Freeman, Frankie Muse, 80, *81*

Garcia, Gustavo, *45*
Godwin, Wendell R., *11*, 12
Gordon, William, *35*
Gray, Garland, 47, *47*
Greensboro, NC, 48, *48*

Hayes, George E. C., *38*
Henderson, James H. M., 23, *23*
Hernandez, Pete, *45*
Hernandez v. Texas, 45
Herrera, John J., *45*
Howard, T. R. M., 61, *61*
Hunt, Nettie, *30*
Hunt, Nikie, *30*

integration, 7, *7*, 14, 22, 39, 47, 48, 49, 79

Jim Crow laws, 5–6, 23, 68, 85
Johns, Barbara, 41, 81

King, Martin Luther, Jr., 39, 60, *84*, 86
Ku Klux Klan (KKK), 6, 58, *58–59*

Note: Page numbers in *italics* refer to images and captions.

Lacks, Henrietta, 23,
Lincoln University (The Ashmun
    Institute), 76–77, *76–77*
Marshall, R. G., *25*
Marshall, Thurgood, 9, *20*, 26, *26*, 27, 37,
    38, 77, 85
Mays, Willie, 57, *57*
Meredith, James, *84*
Milford High School (DE), *64*, 66–67, *67*,
    69, *69*, 70, *70*, 71, *71*, 79–80
Motley, Constance Baker, 80, 82–83,
    82–83, 84, *84*, 85, *85*, 86–87, *86–87*
Murphy, Sarah L., *10*

NAACP Legal Defense and Educational
    Fund, 26, 82
Nabrit, James M., Jr., *38*
National Association for the
    Advancement of Colored People
    (NAACP), 6, 9, 11, 26, 39, 52, 61, 79,
    83, 87
National Negro Network, 15, *15*

Patterson, Robert B., 53
Plessy v. Ferguson, 6–7, 35
polio vaccine, 23
Price, Hugh, *62*, 63–64, 66
Prince Edward County (VA) schools, 40,
    41, 79, *80*, 81

Rayburn, Sam, *68*
Redding, Louis, 69–70
Reed, Stanley, 32, *32*, 34, 37
Regional Council of Negro Leadership
    (RCNL), 53, 56, 61, 68
Robert Russa Moton High School, 41,
    42–43

Salk, Jonas, 23
Scales, Ruth Ann, 72, *72*
Scales, Vivian, 72, *72*
school segregation, 7, 9, 13, *16–17*, 28
    inequality in Black schools, *10*, 11–12,
    40, 46
    student strikes, 41, *42–43*, *80*
segregation, 5–7, 22, 24, *27*, 28, 31–32,
    36, 72, 80

Southern Manifesto, 49
Speaker, Tris, *57*
Speakes, Joy Cabarrus, *40*, 41, 81
Stanley, Thomas B., 44, *44*, 47
Stokes, Sandra "Sandy," *80*

Taft Junior High School (DC), 63–64, 66
Till, Emmett, 68
Todd, Lucinda, 39
Topeka, KS, *8*, 10–12, *13*, 37, 39, 72
Trent, W. W., 75, *75*
Tuskegee Institute, 23

U.S. Supreme Court
    Brown case, 21–22, 24–26
    desegregation cases, 9–10
    unanimous *Brown* decision, 27–28, *30*,
        32, 34–35, *38*, 39
    Warren court in 1953, *28–29*

Vinson, Fred, 21, 22
voter registration, 52, *53*

Warren, Earl, *22*, 24, *25*
    disagreement with Eisenhower,
        24–25, 42
    Supreme Court confirmation, 21,
        31–32, 34–35
    unity on *Brown*, 22, 24–25, 27–29, 31,
        35, 39
White, Hugh Lawson, 51–52, *52*, 53, 56
White Citizens' Councils, 7, *50*, 53, 56, *56*,
    58–59, 61, 79
white supremacist violence, 4, 53, 56, *56*,
    70, 75
Winfrey, Oprah, 18, *18*

About the Author

Selene Castrovilla is an acclaimed, award-winning author. Her five books on the American Revolution for young readers include Scholastic's *The Founding Mothers*. Selene has been a meticulous researcher of American history since 2003. She has expanded her exploration into the civil rights movement, as well as the Civil War, in a forthcoming book. A frequent speaker about our nation's evolution, she is equally comfortable with audiences of children and adults. Please visit selenecastrovilla.com.

PHOTO CREDITS